WHEN YOUR FRIEND IS GRIEVING
Building a Bridge of Love

When Your Friend Is GRIEVING

Building a Bridge of Love

Paula D'Arcy

SHAW

WATERBROOK
PRESS

WHEN YOUR FRIEND IS GRIEVING
A SHAW BOOK
PUBLISHED BY WATERBROOK PRESS
2375 Telstar Drive, Suite 160
Colorado Springs, CO 80920
A division of Random House, Inc.

ISBN: 0-87788-088-3

Copyright © 1990 by Paula D'Arcy
Cover photo © Robert Cushman Hayes

SHAW and its circle of books logo are trademarks
of WaterBrook Press, a division of Random House, Inc.

Library of Congress Cataloging-in-Publication Data

D'Arcy, Paula, 1947-
    When your friend is grieving : building a bridge of love / Paula D'Arcy.
        p. cm.—(The Heart and hand series)
    ISBN 0-87788-088-3 (pbk.)
    1. Consolation. 2. Bereavement—Religious aspects—Christianity.
    I. Title. II. Series.
    BV4905.2.D35 1990
    248.8'6—dc20   89-35360
                                                                    CIP

Printed in the United States of America

02   01

10   9   8 7   6

for my daughter, Beth Starr,
who loved me
through every moment of my grieving,
and for the members of
the First Congregational Church, Watertown, Connecticut
who were the bridge of love that healed me

Contents

Acknowledgments

My special thanks to Lois Lake Church, Theresa Lipeika, and Priscilla Norton—who lovingly discussed their own grief experiences with me, allowed me to quote from their journals, and helped me to edit, add, and delete so that this book might be as widely reflective as possible of those who grieve. Without their help this book would never be complete.

I also thank Cubby Hickox, Judy Helson, Geoffrey Brown, and Eleanor Santucci Flower for the contributions from their own writings.

Those first days, sorrow's pain
was tangible:
an amputation, a dismemberment,
the gap so great, no sobs,
children, friends
would fill its space:
a broken heart is body's pain indeed.
Days pass, and nights, flowing into weeks;
milk no longer spills
with my tears.
Hours once spent weeping
now weave into patterns,
our words of grief and love
now reach for friendship's clasp,
now look ahead . . .

Lois Lake Church
From Quarto, *written for Emily, 8/8/84*

Introduction

During the first months following the death of my husband and child, I locked myself inside my apartment. When the phone rang, I stared at the receiver until it was still. Friends knocked at my door, calling my name, and I wouldn't answer. If my arms could not hold the ones for whom I longed, then I wanted them empty. It was my angry choice—and my own private choice—for I was building hard barriers inside of me. In subtle, secret ways I had begun to say "no" to all of life because part of life had hurt me.

But my friends would not be turned away by my barricades. Their love persisted. To my chagrin they were not satisfied with my "public" faces, nor were they put off by my walls. Gently they kept chipping their way into my life, demanding that I be truly present. They pushed past the shadows where I wanted to hide, and refused to accept the memory-filled, half-life I was choosing. But they did so not by reprimand; they challenged me by loving me.

Stubbornly they clung to their vision of who I was and who I could be, even following such a tragedy. They did what I could not do for myself in my broken state: they held onto the vision that I would heal.

Over a period of time their love for me, and their intent that I again begin to love life back, forced me to choose between two strong forces: my memories, and the fearsome, rough road of loving again. No one grieves without facing that choice. It isn't that we *can't* love again; it's that we *won't*.

Eventually I learned that nothing would preserve my memories more than my willingness to carry the experience of love I had known onto the new roads that lay ahead. I faced the truth that nothing is ours until we let it go. That's the mystery of both life and death. A person is rich if she is surrounded by friends who call her to truth. And richer still if she can be that friend for another.

That's what this book is about—love and support. Designed to instruct and encourage those who want to help a grieving friend, its message is essentially that the bridge to those who grieve can be built only with love. Since love cannot be predicted, these pages cannot contain perfect answers, nor any guaranteed "how to's." But hopefully the experience of hearing about grief through the eyes and hearts of those who have known it will enable friends, like you, to be more sensitive and helpfully supportive during the grief process. When friends learn to recognize some of grief's common faces, and understand the fears behind them, they already have a great advantage.

Because most of my experience with those who grieve has been with women, I have chosen to use the female pronoun in this book. But this is not meant to undercut the feelings and emotions of men. Men grieve, too. And they need every bit as much caring and support from friends.

Grief is the heart's response to any deep loss. For purposes of simplification this book will use the language of personal loss. However it should be clearly acknowledged that the word *grief* is all-inclusive. There are many deaths in life, and we grieve for all of them. We mourn prolonged loss of employment, death of a pet, infertility, death of our dreams, divorce, moving, losses caused by aging and disease. We grieve all endings on the way to new beginnings. And all the griefs change us.

Many of the things I've written about in this book I learned during my own heart's journey through the strange land of grief. Because we credit with authorship the person who has actually put the words onto the page, only my name is listed as the author of this book. But my unnamed co-authors are the hundreds of fellow-grievers I've met over the last twelve years. They have allowed me to step into their hearts and private journeys, confirming my own learning and experience. And they are joined by the friends who made, and continue to build, my bridge of love—the friends who believed in me and accepted me in my sorrow, just as I was, and taught me about unconditional love. This book is our collective gift.

1
Every Grief
Is Unique

No two individuals, no matter how close, and even if they are grieving the same loss, ever grieve in the same way or at the same speed. Every grief is unique.

Grief may:

- provoke tears.
- turn to anger.
- manifest itself as an eagerness and compulsion to talk.
- be stony silence and a refusal even to mention the deceased's name.
- be determined busyness, so there is never time to be alone, or to think or feel.
- appear as withdrawal and an unwillingness to draw close to anyone.
- become an overwhelming need to be held or touched.
- be complete disinterest in sexuality or intimacy.
- be dedication to a cause left unfinished by the deceased.

- surface as total inertia and the inability to initiate or volunteer for anything for a long, long while.
- inspire impassioned devotion to causes related to the loved one's death (e.g. scholarships, memorials, legislative changes, medical research).

And, most confusing of all, it may be all of those things.

Old people and young people grieve differently. Spouses grieve differently. Men and women grieve differently. Members of the same family grieve differently. The same individual grieves successive deaths differently. All grief is colored by who we are when we grieve and the special nature of our own relationship with the one who has died.

There are only two certainties. That those who lose something or someone who was precious to them *will* grieve, and that the healing process begins with love.

In My Own Way

Judy, a mother in Saskatoon, Canada, wrote this after losing her young son:

If I had one request to make of those who came to be with us after our son was killed, it would have been to ask them to let us grieve our way.

When six-year-old Danny died in a farm accident, my husband and I immediately acted out the roles which came naturally for us. While he huddled in a chair in shock and pain, I showed strength in front of others. While he was either lost in another world or shaking with sobs, I appeared dry-eyed.

We did this not by choice, but as the result of our individual natures.

Others were uncomfortable with our coping methods. At first I needed time alone to walk, think, and cry. I wasn't allowed that. Later when I wanted to talk about Danny, most people sat quietly, waiting for a chance to change the subject.

My husband also needed to be allowed to feel pain and cry. When he was overcome by tears, he was fed strong Valium by a friend. The day of the funeral he was told, "You've got to pull yourself together." That same day another person said to me, "You better not have too many of those pills," and refused to believe that I hadn't had any. My husband wasn't supposed to cry. I wasn't crying enough.

However, it wasn't long before our social conditioning molded us into acceptable people with appropriate coping strategies. I cope now by talking with friends, sharing my grief with those who are willing to cry with me. My husband acts the way a man is supposed to act. He talks to no one. He doesn't cry. While I have spent hard months and years crying and talking and working through my pain, my husband is trapped within his grief. And I could weep at that terrible injustice.

There is a sacredness in tears. They are not the mark of weakness, but of power. They speak more eloquently than ten thousand tongues. They are messengers of overwhelming grief, of deep contrition, and of unspeakable love.

Washington Irving

All who have gone through the process of grief can identify with this grieving woman and her husband. Many times friends don't know how to act or what to say. They are uncomfortable with the grief process and with the way the grieving person is behaving.

My Depression—Part of the Grief Process

I have often received phone calls from anxious friends or family members. They go something like this: "We are so concerned about Mary. She still cries all the time and is so depressed since her husband's death. It's been so long now that we feel she needs help."

The caller's tone always implies that Mary's grief is two or three years old. But I ask the most important question, regardless. "When did Mary's husband die?"

And when I'm told, "It's already been two months!" then I know who *really* needs the help—not Mary, but her family and friends!

Depression is a very real and natural part of the grief process. Literally, the body is weeping. But those surrounding the bereaved often become alarmed because such depressed behavior is so uncharacteristic of their loved one. They fear that unless they force a change, this uncharacteristic behavior will become a new, permanent state.

Although the state *is* new, in healthy grief it will not be permanent. It will pass in time, another phase of the grief process. How can you, as a friend, help most? By recognizing depression as a stage, and realizing that it is normal to be depressed as one faces the pain of loss.

Four months after my loss I made this entry in my grief journal:

Everyone is so anxious for me to get better. They don't want me to hurt. But I do hurt, and I need to cry. If I put on a brave face, it only helps them. It drains me.

Deep, uncontrollable crying, and living on an emotional rollercoaster may be the state of affairs for a long time while people grieve. No one learns to love and depend upon someone quickly, nor do we let go of deep attachments with speed. Healing takes time, and sadness and depression are part of the healing process.

Don't Rush Me ... Accept *My* Timetable

Grief is a *process*, not a *competition*. If you can believe that and then convey your patience and understanding, it will be much easier on your grieving friend—*and* on you!

The memories of my own early months of grief are still vivid. My thirty-three-year-old husband and twenty-one-month-old daughter had been killed in an automobile accident involving a drunken driver. I was twenty-seven, three months pregnant with a second child, and holding onto sanity by a thread. No one was sure how to help me, least of all *me*. It should have been enough for me to cope with the enormity of my losses. But I was also sensitive to the discomfort my circumstances created in those around me. I knew life would have been easier for everyone if this tragedy didn't intrude. I knew my needs were overwhelming. But no force of my will could change what I felt like inside.

As the weeks passed, my own impatience to heal was fueled by the impatience of others. I kept telling myself that I must hurry up and get better, that others who grieved healed more quickly, that even with my life in pieces I ought to be controlling the disaster in some way. It was taking me too long.

Inside I was tense and raw—fighting just to make it through the hours. And then well-meaning friends would say, "By now you should be . . ." and I wanted to die inside.

The "By now's":

- By now you should be dating again.
- By now you should be getting out of the house more.
- By now you should be returning to work.
- By now you should be putting those pictures away, doing something with those clothes.
- By now . . .

When those phrases were spoken (every single one of them before I was ready to do what the speaker was suggesting), I used to think angrily, "How do you know? How can you know what I feel like inside? If I don't know, how can you?"

In the past twelve years hundreds of others have echoed the same frustration: Friends were ready for them to be healed and were telling them what they ought to be doing long before they were ready themselves. And that call for the bereaved's life to "return to normal" exerts an extra pressure during an already demanding and difficult time.

Those who grieve need a friend who supports them and their own timetable. As a friend, you can communicate your acceptance of the bereaved's readiness or non-readiness at the various stages of grief. Those who grieve need to make their own choices without fear of criticism.

It simply isn't against the law not to date after having been widowed for over a year. A person can't be arrested for leaving the deceased's clothing hanging in a closet either. Nor is it punishable to continue making regular trips to the cemetery for weeks or months. Whether we admit it or not, most bereaved have a cache of treasured items they choose to keep, or a ritual they don't want to abandon for a long while. As long as there are other good signs of health, growth, and healing, those ties should be left unjudged.

The comments which began, "By now you should be . . ." caused me to feel worse about myself than I was already feeling. It seemed that my life was turned upside down, but nevertheless I was being asked to measure myself against some impersonal standard—to grieve in an approved pattern so that others would feel comfortable. But I couldn't schedule my grief like that.

My friend Glenna saved me from the agony of trying to hurry along my grief in order to please others. One day she asked me, "What difference would it make if you *were* following everyone's suggestions and fulfilling those outward signs of progress?" It was a revealing question because no matter what I managed to accomplish on the *outside* to encourage or satisfy others, I realized I would still be only as far along on the *inside* as I truly was. I could make myself look good to others, but I couldn't change the reality that grief is an individual process, not a fifty-yard dash.

To love is to be vulnerable. Love anything, and your heart will certainly be wrung and possibly broken.

C.S. Lewis

More than anything else, I learned that those who grieve need to be accepting of themselves. They need to measure progress only by examining their own growth, not by comparing themselves to anyone else. As a good friend, accept those who grieve just as they are. Encourage them to be patient with themselves and gently remind them of the progress they have already made. Glenna's acceptance of me just *as I was*, and *right where I was*, moved me farther forward in my healing than the countless other remarks that hoped to hurry me on.

Acceptance coupled with love is a powerful gift.

Something to Think About . . .

Whose timetable are you following in the grief process—yours or your friend's?

2
Embracing Grief

Initially, grief work can be avoided. But not forever. Eventually grief has its due. If grief is resisted and not faced head-on, it simply goes underground and surfaces as a physical problem or a long-lasting emotional distress, such as bitterness or resentment. But the pain of grief should not be faced *only* because hidden grief causes chronic displaced physical or emotional symptoms. Grief should be faced because the seed for healing is found only through embracing grief's pain. It is as if grief refuses to give up its gift of healing until one has felt true brokenness.

The temptation to resist grief is great because the process is so unknown. When someone grieves she feels as if she has been taken to a strange land. Everything on the outside is different and new—but even more unsettling, everything on the *inside* is also unrecognizable. A minute ago life was in order; now it will never be the same.

If those who grieve feel bewildered by their new reality, it is understandable that friends and family will also feel uncomfortable. No one is sure how to help, and everyone has to make adaptations and adjustments.

For the majority of those who grieve, the first year of grief is all-encompassing. For most, the first facing of every holiday, anniversary, birthday, etc., forces sizable adjustments and deep heartache. A year ago the loved one was present. Now life's celebrations must be faced in his or her absence.

Grief is accentuated when basic life skills must be acquired. Many widowers have never cooked or shopped. Both men and women may be afraid to stay alone at night. Some bereaved have no license to drive and are now alone with no means of transportation. Parents whose lives have been totally oriented around a child may have to re-create a daily rhythm and routine because theirs have been shattered. Most of all there is the experience of emptiness. Empty house. Empty arms. Empty heart.

People manage the first days, months, and year in various ways because each individual brings her own family history and emotional nature to the grief process. Some initially will act very much in control. Throughout all the immediate mourning rituals, and in the first weeks that follow, they seem to be themselves. But they are not themselves. Their "behavior as usual" should only alert friends that they aren't yet ready to face the enormous new reality of their loss. It is too large to fit inside.

During the first four seasons following loss, the newness of sorrow and the painful environmental changes are the most difficult challenge. There must be a first time for experiencing familiar observances in light of the new reality. A husband who has lost a spouse may miss their early morning walks together; a mother may grieve over her little girl who's gone every time she sees a child in the supermarket.

Especially throughout this first year the grieving person will show the physical and emotional changes of shock, anger, character change, and moodiness.

Shock

Except in critical situations where professional help is obviously demanded (for example, if the bereaved has a total inability to function or threatens suicide), the shock of grief will wear away in its own time. Soon the bereaved will begin to feel and exhibit the effects of loss. But in the meantime, her immediate refusal to feel the loss is simply the body's way of coping. If you want to help at this time, let shock do its work. Don't urge your friend to "face the facts." If she could, she would.

Others who grieve may weep and fall apart emotionally almost instantly. They will sob through the rituals someone else attends with great poise. But after a time they may well become emotionally spent, feeling a delayed, frozen calm. In whatever rhythm grief occurs, its impact is consuming, and the bereaved have little control over their new behavior. Like a wild and raging fire, grief has its way.

In the first days following my own losses, I remember behaving quite capably. I was dry-eyed through the funeral, and in greeting others even remembered those celebrating birthdays and anniversaries. From all outward appearances, I functioned well.

But today I hardly remember the particulars of those days and events. It was my state of shock, and not my own strength, which allowed me to handle all I needed to then. Shock got me physically through the hours and the rituals. But inside was a great void. What looked good to others was a paper-thin facade—to me, nothing seemed real.

However in three weeks' time, everything changed. By then I was reeling from the force of my tears, anger, despair, and rage. I longed for the great void, but could not re-create it. Grief had found its mark in my heart, body, and soul.

How can you help? Rather than debating whether or not your bereaved friend is in shock (and should or shouldn't be), or whether she needs to face reality or gain control, it is much more fruitful to love her by letting her be. Accept her emptiness or tears with equal compassion, knowing that both exist because of pain. If you hurt simply because she hurts, she will sense it. Open your heart with love, not judgment. When I grieved, I fed on that love.

Anger

If you want to sharpen your ability to love someone unconditionally, then find someone who is grieving! Those who grieve can be very difficult to love. To grieve is to live on an emotional rollercoaster, feeling more out of control of the emotions than ever before. One minute the bereaved can be frustrated with everyone, thinking that all human beings are insensitive and annoying. The next hour she may be weeping because she feels so all alone. Or she may suddenly wish that the insensitive friends she has just thrown out would return and visit.

There are times when those who grieve cannot be pleased. They can only be loved.

When my family was alive, my busy life was filled with loving friends. After my family's death, the same friends called and visited in great numbers, reaching out to me. But even though I often wept because I felt so deserted and alone, I also found myself sitting and staring at a ringing phone, incapable of making myself pick it up. The phone calls might persist for hours while I stared at the wall, unmoving.

I refused countless handwritten invitations. Or I accepted— and then changed my mind at the last minute. Some friends became understandably angry and confused. And in that anger and confusion they were a perfect mirror of what I felt like inside.

I was in the constant throes of an inner storm I couldn't understand. I was more angry than I ever thought I could be because life had dealt me such a blow. I was angry with my husband and child for leaving me; I was constantly looking at

---

Let grief do its work. Tramp every inch of the sorrowful way. Drink every drop of the bitter cup. Draw from memory and hope all that they can offer. To see the things our loved ones have left behind will give us daily pain—the clothes they wore, the letters they wrote, the books they read, the chairs in which they sat, the music they loved, the hymns they sang, the walks they took, the games they played, their seat in church, and much beside—but what would we be without those reminders? Would we like quickly to break with the past in order to assuage grief? Those who truly love will say that they have found in sorrow a new joy, a joy which only the broken-hearted can know.

W. Graham Scroggie, in Billy Graham's *Facing Death*

women with spouses, or families with children, hating everyone who had what I had lost. Those thoughts made me feel even more hateful, and anyone close to me felt the upheaval.

What love it takes to see someone through that storm! As a friend, your suggestions and offers of help may all be dismissed—and maybe quite angrily. You may feel your words went unappreciated. But friends who stick with the bereaved through that storm are life-lines.

None of the phone calls and invitations to me were wasted. Even when the calls went unanswered and the invitations were refused, the fact that my friends persisted was important to me. I might have been angry, but those continuing gestures of love refused to let my anger have the final say. Those gestures showed me that the anger I couldn't control hadn't made me unlovable. Or unlovely. I wasn't hateful; I was in pain.

No one can calculate the worth of a friend's love at such a time.

Character Changes

Those who grieve almost always change and seem "out of character." Grief etches itself deeply in the innermost parts and becomes an all-inclusive spiritual, physical, and emotional upheaval. And yet, knowing this, we are still surprised to see the bereaved changing!

For many, grief is the most powerful and important look they have ever taken at the meaning of life. Grief rearranges priorities and introduces its guests to emotions, passions, and anger to an extent which they never believed themselves capable. Grief is a reckless time. But the changes in outlook and behavior which result from this inner revolution are actually wonderful signs, heralding growth and healing.

However, changes can also become barriers. It's human nature to love what's familiar, even if the familiar is hurtful or needs improvement. Feelings of safety and security are strong compulsions. So often, when bereaved persons suddenly stop living up to their friends' expectations and begin to vary from past patterns of behavior, it strains friendships. And eventually many find new friends who have no past in common with them and, hence, no expectations. New friends can do what is really needed: accept the bereaved right where they are—because they have never known them any other way.

New spouses or dating partners are often difficult for old friends to accept. They are seen as being too different from the deceased. New (perhaps extravagant) behaviors are taken as signs that the bereaved has lost all sense and control. Actually the new behaviors may be the very signs of *gaining* control over life, in some instances for the first time—for when a person finally understands the difference between passing worries and the legitimate, eternal matters of life and death, a new freedom unfolds. But for friends who need the safety of sameness in their world, and those who haven't been opened to freedom by the painful lesson of loss, the bereaved's new perspectives and priorities may be very intimidating.

My friends Jim and Betsy were among the close circle of friends with whom my late husband and I had socialized the most. Our families celebrated many occasions together, and our children played together. But after my loss, I refused most of their early invitations. I couldn't have put it into words at the time because I didn't understand it then. Now I see that I turned them down simply because they were the closest mirrors of what I'd lost. Being with them was just too painful.

Although my refusals to be with them must have been hurtful and confusing, they never stopped inviting me or trying to include me. Their gestures toward me continued *in spite of* my response toward them. Eventually, when I could handle it emotionally, I ventured back to their home. And as I began to date, they included me and the different men I was seeing. Whether or not they silently disapproved of some of my dates (and I'm sure they must have!), they were always welcoming. When I moved from an apartment to a house, they came and helped. They watched me move through change after change in life-style and priorities, and their consistent response was, "We're right behind you!" They *must* have cringed at some of my choices, knowing that I had many things to learn. But I never would have guessed that from their behavior. They watched me change, and they grew with me. They accepted my timetable for grief. And they accepted me.

What a prized quality in a friend: someone who will let you change and will support you through the changes. Not once did Jim and Betsy set themselves up as my teachers to show me the way. They believed in me while I found my *own* way.

Having friends who are willing to stretch in their own lives so that the bereaved isn't condemned to be measured against that person "she used to be" is a marvelous gift. Jim and Betsy understood that people do not return to "normal." One place the bereaved is never privileged to return after she's been visited by deep loss is "normal." There's no such place anymore—nor, am I sure, there ever was. Grief always picks a person up in one place and puts her down in another.

Moodiness

Grief is synonymous with mood changes. One day those who grieve are angry, the next depressed; one day hopeful and welcoming, then annoyed by every intrusion. I wrote in my grief journal:

Tonight I laughed and seemed my old self, and it was the assurance everyone wanted that I'm "me" again. "It's over," they probably thought in relief. But I know that my laughter was not an end to my tears.

It was only a respite.

Tomorrow I may cry again, or be angry, or depressed, or see no hope. I fear my emotions because they fly me back and forth. It's so hard, but that's the way I am now.

I wish others could share my laughter, but not dismiss me with it. I'll need them again tomorrow, without judgment, when the tears start all over again.

I must be terrible to love.

Moods are grief's nature. Because the moods of grief are so strong and variable, you can never let them be your measure of how your grieving friend is doing. Up and down is how she's doing, and how she *will* be doing for a long time. And you, as a friend, must learn not to take the bereaved's moodiness personally.

Loving and helping someone in the throes of such moods requires great understanding and patience. You need a firm resolve not to let your own feelings be hurt by the many swings in mood. I often rudely turned away a friend on Monday whom

I would long for on Tuesday. All the actions that seemed to be harshly directed toward others had little or nothing to do with them. They just happened to be walking through the room when my pain was flying.

It was most difficult to share my fleeting "good" moods, because I feared they would be misunderstood. What if others thought the pain was gone because we had shared one light moment? What if they considered me healed when I was still hurting so?

But most of all it was difficult to share my fleeting "good" moods with *me*. I chastised myself over and over for most of my early moments of levity. How dare I laugh again after that horrible accident?

I needed friends, stronger and wiser than me, who understood that my moods were natural and did not take them personally.

Physical Consequences

How surprised I was to learn that grief was affecting me *physically* as well as *emotionally*. Yet there I was, walking around, feeling as if someone had literally hurled a cement block into my chest. Physically, I hurt: The chest pain was strong and undeniable. " 'Broken heart' is not just figurative language," says my friend Lois. I know she is right.

Grief may cause difficulty in sleeping and eating. It can be a time of weight fluctuation, insomnia or constant sleeping, and heightened susceptibility to illness. The bereaved can become more accident-prone or feel cold all the time, regardless of the season. She may experience gastro-intestinal disturbances, chest pain, and muscle tension. Typically, grief is a time of low reserve because every energy reserve in the body is being called upon to cope with the emotional storm inside.

It helps to advise the bereaved to get extra rest and to avoid unnecessary fatigue. It is not a time to take on strenuous physical activity (this is not the year to hike in the Andes or to crash-diet to lose that extra twenty pounds). The body needs the energy it can usually spare just to manage daily matters. A short amount of regular daily exercise (fifteen minutes or so of walking or biking) may help with insomnia and lagging energy levels. But the physical demand should not be great, or the purpose will be defeated.

It also helps for the bereaved to reduce any stresses which she possibly can. Sometimes friends and family can reduce some of those stresses themselves by taking on everyday chores, or helping with legal matters, for instance.

But it is *not* helpful to offer drinks or drugs to your friend to "soften" the pain. The effect will only be temporary, and sooner or later reality will reappear. The only way to get through grief is to experience it. And you, as a friend, can help to facilitate the beginning of that journey. If the bereaved sees drinking or drugs as her only way to cope, step in and hold her accountable, or urge her to seek professional help.

Your Role as a Friend

Loving isn't easy. Neither is "putting up with" all the mood swings of a grieving person. But it *is* worth the effort. You, as a friend, can help build a bridge of love to the bereaved; you can help her embrace grief as a step toward healing. Friends create the network of safety in which the bereaved can ride out grief's storm.

Something to Think About ...

What emotional and/or physical reactions to grief can you identify in your friend? How are *you* dealing with them?

3
The Friendship Network

No matter what we are doing or how we are feeling, our friends form an important network to all of us. But even the closest of friends can be tempted to stay at a distance when death occurs. Why? It probably begins with the awkwardness we all feel about what to do or say. Friends also may stay away because of an unconscious fear that death is contagious. It's this kind of subconscious thinking: "If I allow myself to witness how fragile life can be, then I admit that the same uncontrollable circumstances may occur in my life as well." And here's the result—with each passing day the staying away creates a greater gulf.

Don't Stay Away

The fears are real. But perhaps your most difficult task as a friend is nevertheless to stay there with your friend and hurt with her. She needs your physical presence. She needs to know that you are there for her.

Before my own grief experience, when I was the anxious friend, I often excused myself from visiting those who grieved by telling myself that death was a private time, a time only for close family members. I rationalized that the bereaved would rather be by themselves.

Then I became the bereaved. And I learned that even though I *did* seek moments of privacy, I also want to be surrounded. And sometimes I had both desires simultaneously! I just *wanted. Period.* I desperately *wanted* from the depths inside of me.

For most, grief is one of the most confusing times they have ever experienced. People who were fully in control of their feelings and attitudes suddenly are not in control. They don't know what to do, say, or be. They hurt—and feel frightened. To grieve is to inhabit a new land, the land that exists deep inside oneself. Those who grieve begin to wonder, "Will I ever be *me* again? Will I ever laugh again? Will I once again know myself?"

Life-Links

It is this inner newness which makes it doubly important for the bereaved person to be surrounded by friends. Friends represent the things in her world which *are* known and familiar, and which haven't changed.

Friends are a sign of the order of daily life, life as it has been. They are the link. And that life-link is the gift that the presence of friends provides.

Following my own family's memorial service, several members of the church we'd been attending came forward to greet me. We were relative newcomers to the congregation, and there were few people whom I knew well. As many persons spoke to me, my friend Jim stood beside me, helping me with names. Thirteen years later I can still picture every face, every person who walked slowly through the line that night. In many instances they had come not because they knew me or my family well, but because they were a part of my community and church. They came because they cared. And I will never forget it.

That night I was in utter shock and total chaos. In contrast, these friends and church members who reached out to me represented what had been stable in my life. By their presence they carried the memory of stability for me until I could find it again. In the best sense, they became one body, symbolizing the surrounding arms of love in my life. And their gift was powerful.

Visiting Tips

Those first visits in the days immediately following a death are your grieving friend's link to her "usual" world. To her, friends are one familiar structure which has not been ripped away. Thus every person who enters the bereaved's new reality helps to foster another step toward healing. So don't stay away.

But here's a tip: Your visit needn't be (in fact, it *shouldn't* be) lengthy unless the bereaved specifically requests otherwise. Stay long enough to drop off a cake or casserole, or to chat for a few minutes. Stopping by for a short time will let your friend know you care without invading her space or privacy.

There is a land of the living and a land of the dead and the bridge is love, the only survival, the only meaning.

Thornton Wilder

When Close Friends Are Pushed Away

It seems bitterly unfair (in fact it *is* unfair), that sometimes the friends closest to the bereaved before their loss can be the hardest to be with afterward. I struggled with these feelings when I first tried to visit my dear friends Jim and Betsy. I just couldn't be around them because the reminder of what our times together used to be like hurt too much. This dynamic may cause such a strain for both parties that the bereaved forms a whole new network of friendships, usually with persons she hadn't known when her loved one was alive.

But the experience of strain between close friends is not fated to be permanent. Understanding what is going on inside your bereaved friend is crucial. If you are willing to look at the problem and figure out the what's and why's of the strain everyone is feeling, the situation will be eased. Otherwise, some friends may sever ties before the mending period begins.

Unfortunately, as mentioned, close friends remind the bereaved most vividly of "the way it was." This can be so painful to face during grief's early weeks that the bereaved consciously or unconsciously pulls away, just to ease the hurt. There is not another phase of grief that requires more compassionate understanding than this one. And it demands it from those closest to the bereaved—from those persons who are also grieving themselves. This requires monumental love and wisdom on the part of these close friends. Although everyone is hurting, these friends are asked to put the bereaved's greater pain above their own.

For the bereaved widow or widower, being in the company of the couple with whom they were the closest foursome can be a biting reminder that the foursome is now one fewer. Parents who have lost a child may find it impossible to face other families who have children of a comparable age, or children who were friends of their own child. Couples who have lost a newborn die inside when they see pregnant women and new mothers. And couples who have just miscarried may find their hopes too bruised and their wounds too tender to be with another couple whose pregnancy is intact. Every situation which forces those bereaved to look into the eye of what they've lost can be unbearable. And it takes time to confront such realities.

Playing the Waiting Game

Some of my own dearest, closest friends had to wait the longest for our ties to reknit. I didn't want it to be that way, but I couldn't push any faster past the pain and fear. Those friends were the mirror of all I had held and lost. I had many tears to cry before I could look into that mirror and know that the reflection was safe again.

So what can you, as a close friend, do? Probably very little but wait. Maintain contact, but understand refused invitations. Those refusals reflect your friend's pain and are no reflection on you. It may be helpful for the bereaved to see members of a close couple separately. I was able to do that with some of the couples I'd been closest to. I needed both friendships and separate male and female companionship, but I couldn't face them together for awhile. Seeing the people individually was less of a reminder and bridged the roughest period.

Do small things with great love.

Mother Teresa

25

If a friend has lost a child, be sensitive about bringing your own children when you visit, especially if your child and the bereaved's child were playmates. Ask the bereaved if she would prefer to see you alone. She may be grateful for your understanding.

Some friendships never knit together again in quite the same way. And this requires in everyone an acceptance of change, and an understanding that the changes cannot take away a second of the joy which "was." Change is not a judgment of yesterday, but a *moving on*. Everything in life is about change.

No Quick Fix-Its, Please

A wonderful impulse of the human heart is a desire to alleviate the suffering of others. But if you choose to help a friend who's grieving, then you must face the difficult reality that grief can't be "fixed." Grief has to be gone through—it *must* be gone through. Experiencing the pain is a necessary step toward healing.

Perhaps nothing is more difficult than offering companionship and compassion without being able to make things better. After visits with your friend, you may leave feeling very disturbed or uncomfortable yourself. You will be acutely aware of someone else's pain, but unable to erase it. And it hurts to be with someone in that pain, unless you know that in unseen ways she is benefiting.

Tell me how much you know of the sufferings of your fellow men and I will tell you how much you have loved them.

Helmut Thielicke

During the early weeks of my grief my cousin Nancy used to get sitters for her children and arrange to spend the day with me. It couldn't have been a thrill to be with me. I had no interest in anyone's life but my own, and the shock of my loss was still so penetrating that I was struggling to display any kind of sociability. One day in particular, Nancy put me in her car and drove me to Newport, Rhode Island for a change of scenery. I remember sitting numbly by the water, knowing that I was drowning even though my feet were planted squarely on the land.

What could it have been like for Nancy to be with such a companion? She must have felt saddened by my pain, but time after time she came back. There was obviously nothing gratifying in those days for her; it was something she did just for me. I'm sure she doubted the effect of her gestures, and I doubt that my aching heart could express much appreciation. But the truth is that it meant more to me than she will ever know.

It is a challenge to love the bereaved. You give, but may gain very little in return. You see pain but cannot remove it. You're asked to love without measuring or needing a response. It is truly an opportunity to see the truth about your own heart and to know, in firm-rooted reality, that shared heartache is always lighter.

Something to Think About . . .

In what ways are you a life-link for your friend?

4
Talking & Listening

Understandably, most friends are timid
when it comes to talking about the person who has died. It seems
ill-advised to share your own memories and personal feelings of
loss. You are visiting your friend in order to help (which some-
how translates into "cheer") her, and you certainly don't want to
depress her.

But your friend is already sad, deeply sad—maybe sadder
than she's ever been. And the fact that someone tries to distract
her by avoiding any mention of her loss does not mask the
sadness inside of her, nor remove it, even for a moment.

The mind of the newly bereaved does not shut off. The loss
is relentlessly with her, twenty-four hours a day. She can *never*
forget her loved one or what has happened. Thus conversations
which speak to that one topic her heart can hear are helpful, not
depressing.

Talk About the One Who Died

Some of the sympathy notes and cards which I treasured the most were filled with the sender's own recollections and feelings of love and loss. And some of the conversations which I remember most fondly were those in which friends talked with me about my husband and child, sharing their own remembrances. Through the eyes of others I saw glimpses of my husband (as a teacher, friend, or nephew, for instance) which were entirely new to me. And in a warm, loving way, it made me feel as if the "knowing" of him wasn't over.

Sharing your own feelings and memories also tells the bereaved that the loss is very significant to others as well. She does not hold the terrible sadness alone. There is a surrounding community which also remembers and cares. So speak about the deceased and say his/her name. The bereaved person needs to hear it. And don't rush to remove pictures and mementos from your home. The fact that you remember and value your memories tells the bereaved that her loved one's life had meaning and won't be forgotten. Such shared memories have incredible sustaining power.

Allow Your Friend to Talk about the Loss

In the months following my losses I felt compelled to tell the story of what happened to anyone who would listen. I repeated the immediate details surrounding my husband's and child's deaths over and over again.

Eight years later my childhood neighbor "Grandma" Wild died. Following her death, whenever I visited my parents, I'd spend an hour or two in the evening sitting with Grandma's widowed spouse. And even though I'd attended Grandma's funeral and had even delivered her eulogy, Grandpa Wild would still begin each visit by retelling all the events surrounding Grandma's death, just as if I didn't know them.

It would have been easy to believe that his advanced age was responsible for his forgetfulness—or even to suppose that he told the story as a sign of his refusal to accept any reality which followed. But since I already had walked on that same road and behaved in exactly the same way, I knew differently. His behavior had nothing to do with age or denial. He repeated himself to any willing listener because he grieved, and those who grieve have an insatiable need to tell their stories.

Bereaved people do not tell their stories in order to *inform* listeners; they repeat the facts in order to *believe it themselves.* When they speak, it is a form of therapy. It is a mental trying-on, an attempt to make an enormous reality fit inside. It's an effort to make themselves believe that the loss has really happened.

The repetitions serve to break up the pain into smaller pieces, to make them manageable. In a sense, the bereaved are molding their pain until it becomes workable, for the reality which is too great to assimilate must be made smaller.

Advertisements constantly encourage us to believe that life can be pain-free [but] to live without pain is a myth . . . to live without pain . . . is to live half-alive, without fullness of life . . . Many of us do not realize that pain and joy run together. When we cut ourselves off from pain, we have unwittingly cut ourselves off from joy as well.

Clyde Reid, in Tim Hansel's *You Gotta Keep Dancin'*

The value of a friend who will listen without judgment to the retelling of the story is inestimable. In effect, that friend is helping the bereaved to confront her pain. The repeating of the story ends when the painful reality it represents can be believed. Again, there are no norms regarding how long this takes. However, when the telling stops, a friend can assume that the loss has finally been comprehended. The bereaved may still not like it, nor accept it. But the loss *has* found its way into her being, and she knows it is real. Then, and only then, can the bereaved move on into the next stage in the grieving process.

Acknowledge the Loss Yourself

Until you grieve it is impossible to imagine the energy grieving requires. It's not without a lot of truth that people proclaim, "Grieving is hard work." It's also why the first year of grief can be a time of uncharacteristic ill health. Every energy resource in the body is called upon to cope with the storm inside. Energy which normally fuels the immune system is greatly diminished.

In the earliest weeks of grief it is undesirable to expend unnecessary energy. And great energy is used when the bereaved, in meeting others, pretends that things are the same, and works hard to avoid mentioning the loss.

Actually, avoiding mention of the loss only makes others feel comfortable—it doesn't help your friend. For the bereaved, it is only an attempt to pretend that nothing has changed. But that simply isn't true. Grief changes everything and everyone. After her child died, my friend Theresa wrote: "We are forever changed. My husband and I both feel robbed of our youth, innocence, and laughter."

I used to fear the first meeting of friends and acquaintances in the weeks following my loss. I dreaded the encounters because so few people would treat me honestly. Had I been wearing a leg cast, they would have known how to respond to my injury with interest and concern. But there I was, wounded and wearing my invisible full-body cast, and no one knew what to say.

Rather than address my loss, people avoided me with their eyes and greeted me with chit-chat. I saw written all over their faces that they didn't know what to say or do. My loss was like a hot coal, and no one wanted to touch it. I was already feeling awkward about myself, and their reactions intensified my feelings.

What I desperately needed was simple honesty. I didn't need my sorrow to be "unmentionable," or for us to pretend that nothing had changed. I was waiting for eye contact and a sincere comment such as, "I'm so sorry about your loss." The words were incidental. It was the truth they addressed that had the power to make a difference.

Once a loss is acknowledged between two friends, the grief is no longer an unspoken subject. For the bereaved, one more difficult hurdle has been overcome. The acknowledgment of the loss bridges a great chasm. The bereaved's new, constricted circle of grief opens to include one more person. One by one, eventually, the world will have to enter.

The friend who meets the bereaved and only offers the words, "I'm sorry," often leaves feeling that his/her comments were

---

Only a poor man can know the riches of suffering.
                              Dominique Lapierre, *The City of Joy*

terribly inadequate and unhelpful. But he/she should understand that words are symbolic. It is the act of talking about the loss (and all that it means in the life of your friend) which is healing.

I am eternally grateful to the friends who listened and offered simple words of love in my time of sorrow—and to those friends who allowed me to talk about my husband and daughter. For me, they were agents of healing on my road to wholeness, and signposts on my journey into God and life and loving again.

A Willing Listener

What do you say when your friend is grieving? You don't have to *say* anything. One of the greatest gifts the bereaved can receive is a friend who is willing to *listen*.

Those who grieve need to talk because talking is a primary means of finding the feelings that are locked in their minds and hearts, and bringing these to the outside, where they can be known. It is the essence of grief work. Over and over again feelings (hurt, shock, abandonment, anger, guilt) need to be discovered . . . accepted . . . and then let go. A person can free herself from feelings which she names and owns, but those feelings which remain unnamed and unrecognized have the power to control from within. In a sense, the grief process is a process of naming.

In the hours after a good listener had allowed me to talk, I never ceased to feel relieved, as if a new supply of energy had been provided. Even though the conversation might have been draining in the immediate moments, and even if it provoked tears, the net result was always renewed strength.

The visitor to the bereaved quickly makes it known by his/her manner whether or not he/she is willing to listen, or has time to spend. Open-ended statements convey a willingness to listen, and leave the bereaved free to respond in any way. For example, you might say, "Paula, I can't imagine how difficult a time this is for you. How are you feeling today? What's going on inside?"

Then sit back and be silent. You have given the cue that you're willing to listen—the opportunity is there. Now it's up to your friend. If your friend does talk, hear her feelings without judgment. In the mere expression of her feelings, so much good is being done. But if your leading question doesn't provoke any sharing, then let it be for that day. Take your cues from the friend you're trying to help, not from your own agenda.

No Easy Answers

Just how do you help your friend? There are no easy answers. But you *can* be a part of your friend's network of support and a link to life outside of grief. As a friend, you *can* show patience and understanding (even when you feel pushed away). And most of all, you *can* be there when your friend needs you to be a good listener.

Something to Think About . . .

When you allow your friend to talk about the one who died, you are a healer—and the bearer of God's love.

5

Things *Not*
to Say

Maybe, like most people, you feel tongue-tied around
your grieving friend. You don't know what to say, or you say
nothing at all, or you say something and then feel that the words
were completely inadequate.

It *is* hard to know what to say—every grief is unique. In this
chapter I want to share with you, from my own experience, things
that people said to me and how they helped (or didn't help). By
exploring together what you *shouldn't* say and explaining the
reasons why, you will develop a keener sensitivity toward your
grieving friend.

"Call Me if You Need Me!"

"Call me if you need me" is always said with love, and I'm sure
with the full intention of following through if the bereaved does
call. And the intention of that phrase *is* appreciated as you speak.
But, unfortunately, grief can be painfully paralyzing. Ten days
following the funeral, when grief is breaking someone's heart,

she may want desperately to talk with you, but be unable to make the step toward the phone.

My friend Lois described this experience perfectly when she wrote in her grief journal, "Sometimes I feel that I am drowning, too far from land to reach anything or anyone, unless someone reaches out first."

The key to helping is that you, the friend, need to be the initiator. You need to make calls yourself, or simply show up, offering to take a walk, or go for a drive with the bereaved. The specifics don't matter as long as your invitation is definite and sincere. The bereaved needs friends to reach out first.

You might say something like this: "I'm free at noontime today. Come and have lunch with me." Or, "How about seeing a movie together this evening, or taking a walk tomorrow morning at 10?" Once you've asked, let the bereaved be honest about whether or not she feels like company, or wants to go out. A visitor can be powerful medicine, and it may be wonderful for her to feel a friend's nearness for an hour. But even if your offer is refused, know that your caring will have mattered. Try again on another day. Above all, don't give up on your friend.

If you are creative, you can come up with specific ways to show your willingness to be available at any time, day or night, or even when you might not guess there is a need. One friend left me a little card with her name and number, and these words: "I want to be called in the middle of the night!" I was touched by her effort to emphasize her availability and willingness to be called during those hours when anyone would hesitate to wake a friend. If she'd only said, "Call me anytime," I never would have.

My friend Jan was especially sensitive to how it feels to be a single parent when your child is ill. Over and over again she stressed her understanding of what it must be like to tend an ill child in the middle of the night, worried about croup or a high fever, and having no spouse with whom to share your fears. "Please don't ever be alone and afraid in that way," she told me. "I would want to come and sit up with you, even if I couldn't do more than lend you moral support." Her concern was so specific that it made her the person I felt most free to call if a night-time vigil ever became unbearable for me to face alone.

"It Could Have Been Worse!"

"You're lucky! It could have been worse! Many others have it so much harder than you do."

What awful words! Phrases such as these make the bereaved volatile, because no one who is newly grieving feels fortunate.

I remember lying in the hospital following the accident which had just killed my husband and child. Visitors to my room would exclaim, "Oh, how fortunate it is that you lived. How wonderful that your three-month pregnancy is still intact. You are so lucky!" I wanted to shoot the speakers on sight.

Considering the whole of a lifetime, I *was* "lucky," and I do consider myself fortunate and richly blessed. Today, thirteen summers later, I give thanks that I lived, and greater thanks that I was pregnant at the time, and that the small fetus was hardy enough to survive. But in 1975, in those immediate moments of my awful nightmare, I was incapable of any thanksgiving, and the last thing I felt was *lucky*. I only knew the hurt. And I needed

---

Where there is sorrow there is holy ground.

Oscar Wilde, *De Profundis*

---

friends to validate that hurt, not belittle it. My heart was broken, and I could feel only the pain.

When someone is grieving, there will always be ample future time for her to consider the size of her loss measured against other human suffering. There will be years for those who grieve to gain a perspective on their good fortune. But in the early moments of hurt, those who grieve don't care beyond the moment. Early grief is not magnanimous. The griever needs to be held, not chided.

"I Know How You Feel"

Meant to express compassion, the phrase "I know how you feel" is guaranteed to trigger resentment in those who grieve. It causes friction because it carries no truth, even if the speaker means it honestly. We can never know exactly someone else's pain. And nothing belittles the bereaved's heartache more than someone who claims to know her unique hurt. It is far better to say, "There is no way I could know how hard this must be for you, but I hurt because you hurt," or words to that effect.

Friends should know that it is not necessary to "know how someone feels" in order to be compassionate and minister to her well. It is only necessary to be kindhearted and responsive. My friend Sandy has been one of the most compassionate friends in my grief, yet she has never lost a child or spouse. But in other ways she has experienced pain in her life, and her sympathy for me flows from those experiences. Pain recognizes pain. Any friend who knows what it means to hurt and feel brokenhearted can reach out to the bereaved and make a difference.

The only ones who can safely say, "I know how you feel" are those who have experienced the same loss. Support groups are built on the principle that a special bonding occurs between those who have experienced similar losses. But even in those instances, the losses are still unique.

When I tell other grieving parents that I understand what they're going through, I am aware only that I know what the nature and horror of the ordeal was for me. I know that the suffering was deep. And because I have lived through it, I hurt that someone else will suffer in that way. I am familiar with the level of shock and the length of the journey. But exactly how it will be for another grieving parent I cannot know. The depth of grief is always private.

"Don't Worry, You'll Remarry," or "You're Young; You Can Have Other Children"

It may very well be true that those who grieve will one day marry another spouse or bear more children. But words about future possibilities have nothing to do with the bereaved's present pain. In fact, such words seem to dismiss it. Suggestions that the bereaved will undoubtedly remarry or have more children deny the enormity of her loss and imply that human beings can handily replace one another.

No aching sorrow over the loss of one child is resolved by the arrival of another child. If only it could be! It is the person *in particular* who died whom the bereaved knew, loved, and now

---

A definition of mercy: Climbing into the skin of someone and feeling and moving and touching with their hands, walking with their feet, seeing through their eyes, hearing with their ears, moving with their feet, beating with their heart.

41

misses, not a child, parent, or spouse *in general*. Human beings are not generic, and we cannot substitute one for another.

The bereaved must grieve for the individual who is gone. As a friend, do not diminish that necessary grief by suggestion that someone else can make the loss "all better" and remove the pain. There are no shortcuts in grief. And that's a hard lesson all of us need to learn.

Something to Think About . . .

Grief is not generic and neither are human beings. How can you help your friend to grieve her unique loss? How can you be more specific in your offers to help?

6
Questions, Questions

When a tragedy strikes, the bereaved goes through many traumas—emotional, physical, and spiritual.

Asking "what if" seems to be a necessary process for some who grieve. The bereaved wonder "what if?" until they can accept *what was*. It's almost as if the human heart must try on every other scenario imaginable before it can accept the one which actually happened. It's a last attempt to change the unchangeable, if only in the mind.

What If?

- What if I hadn't left his room for those few minutes . . . ?
- What if I'd been driving instead of her . . . ?
- What if I hadn't let him go to the party . . . ?
- What if we'd left just five minutes later, or three minutes earlier . . . ?

In terms of actually changing reality, "what if's" are obviously a futile exercise. No one has perfect control over life, and there never is a guarantee that the outcome which led to someone's death could have been reversed if you or I had acted differently. But in the earliest days following an accident or sudden death, it is very tempting to use hindsight, and to believe that even the smallest difference in circumstances *could have*, and *would have*, prevented the loss.

So if your friend expresses a litany of "what if's" in your presence, simply listen and offer love instead of "answers." Friends don't need to react to "what if's," countering them one by one. The bereaved doesn't want "answers"; she just needs to voice her questions. No one can ever know what *might have been*. And when the bereaved is ready, she will accept what *did* happen. However, in the meantime, imagining other conclusions can be an important step toward that final acceptance.

Feeling Guilty

When a loved one dies, those who survive often review their relationship with that person. And, inevitably, because no human relationship is without some moments of disharmony and friction, the bereaved begins to experience feelings of regret and guilt. She remembers times when she was cross or demanding. She dwells on past mistakes. She recalls moments of frustration

---

Life breaks us all and afterward many are strong at the broken places.
Ernest Hemingway, in Max Cleland's *Strong at the Broken Places*

44

and anger. She asks herself if she did all she could have done. Was she loving enough? Did she spend enough time? Were there signs she should have recognized earlier (e.g. hints of illness), steps she should have taken? Basically, a survivor berates herself for not being perfect. No one ever feels she has done enough, or been enough.

If your bereaved friend feels guilty and says so, let her talk about her guilt. Many bereaved feel responsible, even though no reasonable circumstances support that feeling. Some, like myself, simply feel guilty about being the survivor. It was a long while before I named that feeling inside of me. But my initial question to the universe, "Why did they die?" insidiously became, "Why did I live?" The guilt of being a survivor is especially traumatic when grandparents experience the death of an infant or a young child. Since their lives have been nearly fully lived, they may anguish that they remain on earth while a young life ended so early. These feelings are heightened when the grandparent is very aged and/or infirm and might even have welcomed death for herself. She might say to herself, "I've lived my life. Why wasn't it me?"

Working through guilt means an ultimate acceptance of life's mystery and impartiality. It also means that survivors must forgive themselves for not being perfect, and must accept that each of us can only do the best we can do at any given moment. Many who are torn by guilt are comforted by this prayer:

God grant me the serenity
to accept the things I cannot change,
courage to change the things I can,
and wisdom to know the difference.

Reinhold Niebuhr

There is no changing the past. The only thing we can change is how we live today.

God's Will?

The heart torn by loss always searches for some explanation, a reason why life is so unjust and unfair. And the pursuit of reasons "why" can be very passionate. Having lost a daughter by suicide, my friend Priscilla writes, " 'Why?' is a cry of pain from the soul for which there is no answer." But anyone who has grieved knows that the cry is real.

The desire to understand the loss is great for friends as well. Thus numbers of well-intentioned friends will rush in during the early weeks of grief to assure the bereaved that her loss either was (or wasn't) God's will. In particular, the clergy often hope to sustain the bereaved by offering theological explanations. But the plain truth is that there is no explanation which satisfies raw pain.

When I was given Scriptures and verses in the early days of my grief, I wanted to shout, "No! Not now. I'm not ready. Please come back later." First I needed to be free to hurt—and, possibly, to be very angry with God. I had to be free to wrestle with every prior belief and value, including who God was, and why horrible circumstances are permitted in our lives. I needed to weep and be human. I needed to ask "why" over and over again before I could even consider any answers. I needed to embrace my brokenness before I could mend it.

When it was time to beg theology for answers, believe me, I searched. On my own I initiated months' worth of questions. But not before I had first believed that the whole chaos had even happened to me—that it was real at all, never mind by whose will or act.

The clergy and friends who helped the most did so by loving me. Rather than imposing beliefs *about* God, they offered me the love *of* God. It's impossible to describe the difference in effect, except to say that those who loved me with God's love freed me to cope with God in my own time and in my own way.

I eventually concluded that just because God wasn't the God I had imagined, or thought I wanted (i.e. a God who prevented pain and tragedy), God was still real, still good, and still loving. I had to let go of my narrow image of who God was, or should be, and get to know God as he is. I couldn't have borrowed that conclusion from anyone, no matter how much I trusted and respected them. I had to meet God in my own dark night.

It may take a long while for bereaved persons to sort through the questions of theology. If they haven't embraced previous personal theology, there is everything to hear and consider. And if they've had strong, former conclusions, there is everything to review. But the faith that arises from a deep, personal search inspired by grief is often deeper and stronger than a faith which has never been questioned.

Realize that your grieving friend will have to find her own answers concerning God's will. She cannot borrow yours. How-

---

It is sometimes only through suffering that we begin to listen to God. Our natural pride and self-confidence have been stripped painfully away, and we become aware, perhaps for the first time, of our own personal needs.

David Watson, *Fear No Evil*

ever, if your answers fill you with truth, then when she is ready to search, chances are that she will seek you out.

Living with Questions

One entry in my journal for September, 1975 reads:

> My mind is filled with questions. I feel as if the questions have taken over the inside of me. I wonder if they will drive me mad. Where are my loved ones now? Will Sarah grow up or stay twenty-one months old? Are she and Roy together? Do they miss me? Will I catch up with them one day, or will I always be left behind?

I re-read that entry now, thirteen years later, still able to feel what it was like to be the young woman who needed answers so badly. She would have killed for answers. But in the end, most of my questions, my tormentors, had no specific answers. There was no day of clarity, of definite knowing. In the end, there was God—and that was the answer.

God's presence eventually assured me that my loved ones are safe and well. Perhaps they are still learning, as I am learning. Perhaps they grow, as I do. But certainly they are filled with God's light, and when we meet again, we will recognize one another. There is no more that I am anxious to know. Mystery and I have made our peace with one another.

If I accept the sunshine and warmth, I must also accept the thunder and lightning.

Kahil Gibran

Your friend who grieves lives with questions, doubts, and fears. She wrestles with the mystery of life and death. As a friend, listen to her anguish-filled questions. Support her in her search. It is the power of such questions which lead many to know God intimately for the first time. Encourage her to cry out. But do not fill her with *your* answers: every person must find his or her own.

Prayer Power

As I consider my own long journey through grief, I now realize that I was guided every step of the way—not by burning bushes, or "still, small voices," but by God working through wonderful, sensitive friends, in insights, in writings, and in the tremendous opportunities which have filled my path. And if I was able to avail myself of the help friends offered, and the teachings and opportunities life presented, I believe it was because so many people were praying for me.

"I'll pray for you" is not an idle comment. Friends who said this to me actually fulfilled the commitment. And the light and spirit generated by their prayers surrounded me and gave me every advantage to heal. I will always believe that. I did not do it alone.

Neither did Joe Bayly. He wrote the following in *The Last Thing We Talk About* (David C. Cook, 1969):

I was sitting, torn by grief. Someone came and talked to me of God's dealings, of why it happened, of hope beyond the grave. He talked constantly. He said things I knew were true.

I was unmoved except to wish he'd go away. He finally did.

Another came and sat beside me. He didn't talk. He didn't ask me leading questions. He just sat beside me for an hour or more, listened when I said something, answered briefly, prayed simply, left. I was moved. I was comforted. I hated to see him go.

So pray for those who grieve, because prayers generate power. Pray that your grieving friend will learn to transform her pain into a new freedom, an experience of life's richness and beauty. When grief is transformed, everyone is changed. And mourning is turned into dancing (Psalm 30:11).

Something to Think About . . .

You cannot force your answers on your grieving friend's "what if's?" But you aren't helpless—you can pray. And through prayer, everyone is changed.

7

Specific Ways
to Help

Not everyone in the bereaved's circle of friends is close enough or comfortable enough to be the friend who listens or talks about the deepest feelings and hurts. But such friends still want to help, and indeed they can help. Love comes in many forms.

How grateful I was to those who "loved" me by offering rides (to and from church, doctor's appointments, etc.), by shopping for emergency grocery items or prescriptions when I couldn't get out at night with a new baby, or babysitting at other hours so I could change my scenery for a while, by inviting me to play tennis, dropping off magazines for me to look through, leaving flowers to brighten my day, offering to go with me to functions that were difficult to face or attend alone. In fact my neighbor, Doug, saved my sanity the second Christmas of my grieving by helping me put up a small tree after I struggled to do it on my own. (Ask anyone who has faced that task alone at the emotionally charged holiday time. There may be no greater act of friendship!) The list is endless.

These "helps" are the bounty of friends who might not be in a close circle of listeners. In his or her unique way, each of these friends can help the bereaved person keep the outside structure of her world together. Both the inner and outer worlds of those who grieve need love and attention.

How can you help? There is a variety of ways in which you can lend your friend a practical hand.

Plan Your Visit

The timing of a visit to the bereaved can be a visit's most vital variable. Any close friend wants to be present when the bereaved faces her roughest moments. But that coincidence may happen only by chance. However there is a way to time your visit so that you greatly increase the likelihood that your stay will be beneficial. Very simply, time your visit with the bereaved's schedule in mind, not your own.

For example, to give a grieving mother a chance to talk, visit when her children are in school, or when pre-schoolers are napping. If your friend is part of a family, avoid Sunday, when most family members are home, and there will be the least privacy. However, when the bereaved has been left without family, then consider Sunday. Under those circumstances, Sunday can be a long and lonely day which seems never to end. Basically, it just requires a little thought to find the right time. If you ask the bereaved which days and times are best, or when it's hardest to be alone, then you can orient your visits with much greater sensitivity.

My friend Ann used to call me once a week to see if my new baby, Beth, was in bed. When Beth was asleep, Ann would come and spend time with me. The time was uninterrupted and private, and Ann had found out that nighttime was the time of day I'd prefer a visit. How did she know? She simply asked me. Had she come at 4 P.M. when Beth was hungry, cranky, and needing my attention, I never could have talked to her as I did. Her gesture of fitting in around my schedule spoke volumes to me about her love and genuine caring.

Many nights Ann and I sewed together and hardly talked at all. Other evenings we never picked up our sewing. But regardless of how we spent the hours, it was an evening to look forward to each week. And if I felt like talking, the hours were truly usable.

It's important to add that in the early weeks of grief, when the bereaved's mind races non-stop with the reality of loss, brief visits are greatly appreciated. I remember that as time went on, and I felt more like having company, I often urged someone to stay longer. But it was much easier to say, "Please stay a little longer," than it was to find the words to ask someone to leave.

Run Errands

Friends should not hesitate to ask if there's a specific errand to be run, or a handyman job to do. And the friends who are easiest to call upon are those who are most definite about their willingness and availability.

Once you're real you can't be ugly, except to people who don't understand.

Margery Williams, *The Velveteen Rabbit*

For instance, I loved it when someone would say to me specifically, "I'm free on Thursday morning from 9 to 11, and I'd like to do something for you then. What could it be?" Or, "I'd like to take you to your next doctor's appointment. When is it scheduled?" When friends were that specific, I knew that they were serious about wanting to help, and that they had the time. By indicating their free hours or mornings, they eliminated my fear that I'd ask for help and they'd say yes out of pity or guilt even though it was really inconvenient. I knew if they were making a specific offer, they must be willing and available.

Allow Reciprocal Favors

In time, if your friend offers, it's also important to let *her* reciprocate with a favor. When a person is only receiving help and never giving it, her self-image lowers. So if the bereaved offers to help you, or asks questions about some of *your* struggles, share a little. Even though she is hurting badly and may be more in need of support than you are at the moment, it's still important for her to feel that in some measure she can be a friend in return.

My own losses were so enormous in the eyes of my friends that they felt whatever they were facing was insignificant in comparison. It took me a long while to convince them that heartache is heartache, whatever its size or source, and that I felt left out and isolated if they were never going to feel that they could complain in front of me again. I'd been robbed of enough. I didn't want to be robbed of the chance to be a good friend as well.

Bring a Gift

It's natural to wish to "bring something" when someone is grieving. Friends instinctively want to fill the emptiness. Or maybe they want to touch the pain with something that might help to soften it, even for a few moments. But many find it difficult to decide what is appropriate to bring.

A book is a good idea only if it's carefully chosen and isn't very long. The reality is that most who grieve simply lose their power of concentration. Even avid readers find the period of grief to be a time when reading is no longer a comfort because of their inner distractions. A tape of soothing music (which requires no concentration) may be a healing gift for those who are touched by music's power.

I was very moved by some lovely personal gifts—perfume, a pretty nightie, a new sweater. This may seem contradictory, since during that time I certainly couldn't have been less concerned with fashion or my appearance. And yet the new and feminine gifts made a statement to me. They told me that even though I didn't feel beautiful, I could still receive and wear something beautiful. My femininity had not died with my spouse. And that outward sign, the gift, was the symbol of the femininity I would catch up with again in a future time. Such a gift need not be expensive. Nice soaps, body lotion, or sachets all convey the same meaning.

Flowers are wonderful because they fill the very air. Immediately following a funeral there are always many bouquets of flowers. So if you'd like yours to arrive at a different time, do a little calculation. Estimate when the funeral bouquets will wither, wait a few days, and *then* send flowers. These unexpected gifts will continue the flow of love and support for a longer period.

Six months later, when grief has privately intensified and the larger support system has naturally diminished, it's wonderful to send flowers again. It says that you continue to remember.

Office mates of my friends Allan and Lois gave them a magnolia tree to plant in their garden in memory of their infant daughter, Emily. For years this thoughtful gift will speak of the love of friends, and the beauty of Emily's memory.

Even a single rose, especially on a holiday like Valentine's Day, helped me still to feel included in the celebrations enjoyed by everyone else. A friend's flower could not replace the flowers I might have received from my husband. But still I had been remembered by someone, and it helped a great deal to ease the pain of that day.

A journal is a wonderful present if your friend has any inclination to write. Keeping a personal journal not only is a way to record facts which will fade in memory (in spite of the strongest resolve), but it can become an important record of progress. It is proof of growth in the grieving. It is also an effective way of getting in touch with feelings. Once something has been written down and then re-read, its clarity is twice as great.

In my own journal I often went for days without writing. One entry contained only four words, "I hate my life." But that page was accurate, recorded history for that day. When I began to reach out to life again, I could see how I had made progress from my despair.

A journal is also therapeutic because it is a private, confidential place to record the strongest feelings (like anger) without incurring anyone else's judgment or reaction. It's a safe place to fantasize or yearn. Eventually, when bereaved persons write positively as well as negatively about their lives, the written words reinforce the power of the positive thoughts. As entries are re-read they help to build a new hope.

Give Time

Time is also a precious gift to offer. Time to help with errands, meals, or other children. Time to take a walk once a week. Time to go together to the theater. Time to spend on the anniversary of a birthday or wedding. Time to help fill a long Sunday afternoon, or a weekend evening. Time to be a babysitter, relieving a tired mother or father, perhaps freeing them to attend an important function. Time to help address thank-you notes, or to help with correspondence. Time to help a single parent make decisions when the perspective of another adult is badly needed. Time to take a fishing or camping trip with older children who've lost a parent. Time to help young children pick out Mother's or Father's Day cards, or gifts for a single parent.

Know-how

The organizational skills or "know-how" of a friend are wonderful gifts: for example, your understanding of insurance forms, probate, or taxes. You might be able to provide a hand with storm windows, help with snow shoveling, or give handyman advice.

Let there be no purpose in friendship save the deepening of the spirit. . . . And let your best be for your friend.
Kahil Gibran

My friend Kit mowed his neighbor's lawn when they were out of town to attend a family funeral. When they returned, tired and beaten, their yard was in perfect order. What a boost for a weary morale!

These are the nitty-gritty needs of existence, and while they may seem small, they can be devastating when faced alone. I lovingly remember the friends who called me during snow-storms or hurricanes, realizing that facing storms alone may be scary. Their calls were the simplest and smallest gestures, like the plate of cookies I once received on the anniversary of my child's birthday. But I have never forgotten any of them.

Suggest Activities

Be a support when the bereaved is ready to leave her grief by suggesting projects, involvements, volunteer work, etc. It starts with small first steps, and they are all hard. So let some of the suggestions for moving forward include yourself. Say something like: "Let's take a course together at Midvale College next summer." Or, "Let's purchase some season tickets together for Arena Theater." And, "Join me at my church or club meeting on Friday nights."

Offer to accompany your friend to church. Those who grieve often find it difficult to attend religious services because it is a time when strong emotions rise quickly to the surface. Ironically, as a result, the comforting place of worship may be difficult to attend. Going with someone else helps immeasurably, especially if that friend is sensitive enough to understand that the bereaved might like to sit near the back so she can leave quickly, or possibly a bit early.

The Gift of Touch

Above all, give the gift of touch. No one knows its importance more than the elderly who live alone, or widows and widowers who are by themselves. Those who grieve long to be touched. And it's a wise longing, because the human touch heals. Hugs transfer energy. They break past the aloneness and the isolation, gradually filling the emptiness. So reach out to those who hurt. Embrace them. Transfer your strength.

Something to Think About . . .

In what specific, practical ways will you show love to your friend this week?

8
Help for the Holidays

It's impossible to predict which holidays will be the most difficult to celebrate following a loss. We are all unique. However, it is generally true that the first one or two celebrations of each holiday without the deceased are extremely painful times. And when death has occurred *on* a holiday, or in close proximity to one, that day never again will be free of a mixture of joy and pain.

Here's what Eleanor, a bereaved parent, had to say about the holidays:

I push my shopping cart through Zayre, K-Mart, wherever; sometimes I'm not sure which store I'm in. "Oh, there's the yarn—I'll get green, red, and white." I toss them all into my cart on top of a Thanksgiving Day card for my uncle, or did I send him one already? Oh, well, it will go to someone, some Thanksgiving.

This was a good day for me—I finally found a pair of jeans that fit me since I've gained the pounds from nervous eating.

I stop, watching the activity around me. Decorations are all over, there are none at home. Music is playing happy tunes—no music plays at home. People are buying presents, and the kids finger the packages of candies and stare longingly at stacks of toys and games. No one even notices me—that I seem to stare blankly and wander listlessly, feigning an interest in material texture. "May I help you?" asks the clerk. "No, I'm just looking."

I feel there is a neon sign on my head flashing, "Bereaved parent—handle with care," but no one sees it. Business as usual. They don't know I ate out of desperation because I could not cure my son. Nothing could save him. They don't know that I crochet yarn fast so I can keep my hands busy so my mind doesn't think. I can create something out of yarn, and my child loved my creativity—but nobody here knows my son is dead.

Where do I send my creations? Nobody notices tear-filled eyes as I look at cards that read "Merry Christmas, Mom"—that card won't ever come anymore. Would store security be called if I began to sob and cry out loudly, "Stop the world please, if only for a minute, in respect for my son. He is dead." But I look like an ordinary person.

The First Holidays

As the bereaved anticipates the first holiday she wonders, "How will I behave? What will it be like? What adjustments must be made?" She may dread the day and struggle to find a way to cope with it.

But the first year, though difficult, usually is somewhat softened by the presence of shock. In some ways, the bereaved is still numb. And it may well be the second year, when stark reality intrudes, that the deepest anguish can be felt. It hurts to go through a time meant to be joyful when one is only experiencing pain, realizing that the loved one will never be there to celebrate holidays again.

So don't assume that once the bereaved has made it through the first year she is past the worst. Equal if not greater compassion may be needed in the year which follows. Don't stop reaching out too soon.

But regardless of whether the first or second holiday without that loved one is most difficult for your friend, encourage her to celebrate every holiday in the ways that are best for her. If necessary, support her need to change the way things "have always been done." Let her know it's okay not to function as usual. It's okay to take care of herself, and not to do what is comfortable for everyone else. It's okay to make changes. Help the bereaved arrange what will best get her through these very difficult times. Remind her that any new arrangements she makes are not forever binding. She can always return to traditional ways of celebrating in future years.

Ways You Can Help

Regardless of whether or not the manner of celebrating a holiday changes, the holidays will be different for those who grieve. It's not a matter of whether or not the day will be painful, but how

> *A death blow is a life blow to some . . .*
> Emily Dickinson, *The Complete Poems of Emily Dickinson*

the bereaved will best manage the pain. Encourage your friend not to overextend, to plan her holiday strategy well in advance, and to feel right in doing what helps her the most. Encourage her to acknowledge and accept her feelings, not setting unreasonable expectations that everything will be the same, or that she will feel joyful.

It's important for the bereaved to feel that it's permissible, if it happens, to have some fun, too. Good moments are not a betrayal of the person who died. Moments of fun are life-giving for overextended systems. And moments of happiness are really the greatest tribute to the deceased. Those moments say that those who have died will be remembered and live on not only in tears, but also in joy.

As a friend, you might offer to help out with holiday shopping. Many parents who have lost children find it extremely difficult to enter toy stores in order to purchase gifts for other children on their lists. Sometimes just facing the holiday decorations and hearing carols play is too difficult. It may help for you to accompany your friend on such shopping trips. You might want to shop in stores in neighboring towns, stores which are less familiar and not as filled with memories. Or, if your time is limited, your gift may be as simple as offering to help a grieving friend shop through catalogs.

For all the years that I lived in Connecticut, following my second-year disastrous effort of trying to put up my own tree, my friend Charlie cut down a tree for me, delivered it, and put it up. There will never be a Christmas when I don't remember Charlie and his wonderful way of helping me make it through those holidays. Charlie's gift was unique. Not every holiday gift comes wrapped in a package.

Specific Holidays

We've talked in general about how difficult the holidays can be. What can you, as a friend, do to help? Here are some practical suggestions for those special days.

New Year's is difficult for many because it signifies a new beginning. For those who long for past loves and look ahead to see no desirable new beginning, this holiday accentuates their loss. The reality that life goes on weighs heavy. Others are partying, and the bereaved is going on alone. Three hundred and sixty-five days—empty, unwanted days—stretch themselves out ahead.

You might help by encouraging your grieving friend to break New Year's down into smaller pieces. Instead of considering the long year ahead, suggest that she make a commitment to face one day at a time. While the entire year may not seem bearable, it *is* possible to cope with twenty-four hours at a time.

Valentine's Day, or any day especially dedicated to couples, is harsh for those who are suddenly alone. They may feel distanced from the mainstream of life and cheated out of some of life's richness. There is no relationship for them to celebrate anymore. Thus any small remembrance on that day will help them feel included. When you remember your grieving friend at this time, you communicate that you remember the lost loved one as well. It won't be the remembrance for which your friend's heart longs, but it will still matter. My own piano used to be lined with Valentine cards from caring friends. Each card and remembrance became a visible string of love.

Mother's Day and *Father's Day* are particularly hard when a child has died. It is also important to remember that a widow or widower with small children has no spouse to initiate the celebration. Men who have lost children can feel an especially poignant grief on Father's Day since in our culture today men's identities and masculinity are so tied to providing for and protecting women and children.

Help the bereaved on these days by sending a simple card or note of remembrance. Particularly when parents have lost an only child, your note will show that you understand a very important fact: parents are still mothers and fathers whether their children are with them or not.

After losing her only child in early May, Theresa remembers, "I was so angry not to be remembered on Mother's Day, except by my brother, who bought me a pocketbook. I cried all day. I just didn't know what to do with myself."

Remember as well that you might help on Mother's Day or Father's Day by helping younger children purchase or create a gift for their single parent.

Thanksgiving, Christmas, Hanukkah, and *Rosh Hashanah* are peak times for family celebration. They stir feelings of anticipation in everyone, and a sense that our longings for happiness can truly be fulfilled. For those who grieve, the great disparity between the pain in their hearts and the expectation and merriment of the season can be terribly hurtful. Changing the normal rituals of celebrating is helpful for many. But expect that there will still be pain.

It's a Family Affair

When parents have lost a child, or when a parent dies, the grief is shared by every surviving family member. In the loss of a parent, attention to both the spouse and children is fairly evenly shared. However, in the loss of a child, more attention may be focused on the grieving parents than on surviving siblings.

When a sibling dies, it is a confusing and tumultuous time for surviving brothers and sisters. And because the parents who normally support them through such crises are in need of comfort themselves, needed help may not be adequately given.

Siblings, as well as bereaved parents, experience anger, guilt, fright, and loneliness. The loss is likely their first major facing of life's unfairness. Powerful emotions may rage within, and they may be poorly equipped to acknowledge or release these feelings.

It is common for children to feel like failures because they can't make their parents "better," or because grief over a brother or sister seems to indicate that the live child's presence is no comfort or has little meaning. Many wonder if they, too, will die.

Friends or other relatives can be invaluable by stepping in and supplementing some of the attention that may be missing from shattered parents. If the family is willing, you might arrange to take siblings out of the home for a change of scenery, or an afternoon's activity. Always provide time to listen. Let the children know that talking with you about their brother or sister is okay. Hug them and let them feel loved. Remember them on

---

The hands of those I meet are dumbly eloquent to me. There are those whose hands have sunbeams in them, so that their grasp warms my heart.

Helen Keller, *The Story of My Life*

special occasions which may not be receiving the usual celebration at home. Help them to celebrate holidays which their parents may be unable to face. In a sense, the surrounding adults can become a vital extended family.

Even More Practical

Not only is it important for your grieving friend to *receive* love and support, it's also necessary for her to give it. You might suggest to your friend that you will help to put into practice the following idea: doing something for someone else at the holiday time in honor of the loved one. It's one of the best ways to transform grief at a time of celebration.

My friend Betty lost her daughter, Megan, in 1974. Each year at Thanksgiving, Betty and her family pack a food basket for a needy family in Megan's memory. The basket not only helps another family, but it gives the love Betty's family has for Megan a new road to travel. And that's the essence of healed grief, and the path to health and wholeness for the entire family.

Doing something for someone else could also be family-oriented. Lois and Allan's family remembers their daughter, Emily, with a family Christmas tradition. Each member makes a tree ornament for Emily, symbolizing their remembering. This act doesn't reach beyond the family but reaches into it, encouraging healing from within.

Coping with holidays is never easy for those who grieve. But holidays can be transformed into a time of family growth and outreach. And, as a friend, you can encourage the healing steps that lead back to joy and life.

Something to Think About . . .

What can you do for your grieving friend during the next holiday?

9

The First
Two Years

The progress of grief is so difficult to judge by appearances. A good day may be followed by two weeks of wrenching tears and anger, anger that the bereaved and everyone else assumed was in the past. But this pattern of back and forth, advance and retreat, is the complex nature of grief.

Even when grief looks like a series of regressions, ground that has already been gained is never lost. Every small victory is indelible. Grief is a process of small victories building upon each other until the day when victories dominate.

The Pattern of Grief

Grief which goes up and down, back and forth, is actually healthy. Sustained victories would be unrealistic, and sustained pain would be too severe to bear, so nature protects the griever with this pattern of regressions and advances.

For some reason, the pattern of temporary retreat is often especially pronounced five to six months following a loss. The greatest shock has begun to wear off by then, and the impact of new life without the one who is gone seems to settle in with a new intensity. At the same time, the extra attentions which surrounded the newly bereaved are also diminishing. Life is now seen as it will really be, and the vision can be grim. All of these factors create a period of new despair.

At this crossing my friend Theresa wrote in her journal, "I *can* go on without him. How dare I? But I can. I feel like a betrayer."

Such new realizations tear the heart. And this is why, after seeming to "do so well" for so many weeks, the bereaved may suddenly seem to be struck a second time. If you understand that this isn't a step backward, you can give your friend much needed support. The period is really a tear-filled step forward, a fresh and necessary working through of the reality which exists.

My friend Lois wrote the following words, from the perspective of a grieving person:

Don't be hurt if I can't share in your joy (wedding, new baby, child's milestone) in my usual way. Any ceremonial occasion can make my pain sharper.

Don't be surprised if another, smaller loss makes me react out of proportion to the cause (e.g. a pet's death after a spouse's)—the new hurt can summon up all the pain of the first major loss.

Please understand if I'm oversensitive, touchy, or prone to misinterpreting your words or gestures.

Please be patient if it takes me an extra-long time to finish a task—
with a lack of energy and focus.

I am doing the best I can.

It is extremely helpful during this period to reassure the bereaved that she is not falling apart, or permanently regressing. She needs to hear that this is yet another phase of the grief journey.

In fact, this is a vital phase, for until the pain of grief is faced squarely, the inward parts will not fully heal, and lasting progress won't be made. The bereaved reaches this difficult plateau, and cries these harder tears, because of the strength of the grief work which has already been done. The new tears will move her inward again for awhile, but eventually she will move forward once again.

Not the Time for Major Decisions

In spite of the fact that grief is personal and people are unique; in spite of the fact that one person's solution can be another's undoing; in spite of the fact that there is no single answer about how to grieve or when to put the deceased's clothes away, remove a wedding band, etc.—there *is*, nevertheless, one universal and trustworthy rule which applies to all who grieve: *Encourage the bereaved not to make any major decisions or changes for a year whenever it is possible.*

Even those who think they are functioning well during the first year of grief are still not functioning with complete clarity. The devastation of loss is always accompanied by some level, however subtle, of shock. Judgments are skewed. And it is the rare individual who makes the same caliber of choice during that time that she would make otherwise. Or that she would make in a year's time.

The first year is a time to settle and wait, not forge ahead. Friends and family who are informed can protect the bereaved by encouraging her to wait one year before making changes whose effects may be important or long-lasting.

During my first year of grief, in fact in the first weeks, I allowed myself to plunge into decisions where the proverbial angels would have feared to tread. My simultaneous loss of a husband and child alone merited me a high-risk score on any psychological stress chart. Add the realities of my pregnancy, my own memories and injuries from the accident, and a major change in financial status. Then add shock. Would you have advised me to take on major choices? But I did.

In a one-month period immediately following my losses I moved from my residence, away from all of my friends. In fact, I moved out-of-state. This meant I had to pack all of my belongings, half of which I gave away on the spot. I gave away treasured items as well as expensive and useful household equipment. I believed then that I would never again live in a house, never need a lawn mower, ladder, etc. So I sorted, gave away, and threw away.

Before three more months had passed, I knew that the decision I'd made to leave my familiar surroundings was no longer right for me. So at great expense (and emotional strain) I removed my furniture from storage, packed again, and moved back to my former town. In the three months I'd been gone, I had struggled in a new state with unfamiliar pharmacies, doctors, and a new driver's license, registration, and insurance. It had been too hard. Finally I realized that I would go mad inside if at least my surroundings weren't familiar.

But because of my initially hasty decision to move, I was now minus many things I had treasured or needed, in some cases never remembering how or why I'd dispersed of these items. At the time when the decisions were made, I had looked and seemed quite in control. But appearances can be so deceiving.

The wisdom in waiting a year is that the bereaved person gives herself the greatest opportunity to get back both to an inner and an outer equilibrium. So advise your friend to take things slowly. The inner pain tempts those who grieve to believe that if they make changes (for example, move or change homes), the reminders will be fewer, and the pain less. But the truth is that the turmoil and pain the bereaved feels will go with her wherever she goes. There is no place to flee. No place will be truly "right" until she is right. She won't be free until she works through her pain, and progress actually will be speeded by grieving in a familiar place. The "loss" of familiar surroundings can become an additional grief.

As a friend, you also need to caution the griever against making hasty decisions even in the immediate hours surrounding death. The pain is so acute then that those who grieve often boldly decide to get rid of things, as if the act will excise the hurt. My friend Theresa illustrates this tendency:

When Ronny [her nearly two-year-old son] first went into the hospital for his cancerous tumor, I longed to get back to his room and touch his toys. I longed to remember how his bed and clothes smelled prior to his illness.

But when we knew his death was imminent, and before we returned from our long hospital stay, I asked my mom if she would go to his room and remove everything. Suddenly I couldn't tolerate the thought of any reminders.

She did a thorough job. She changed beds and washed clothes, even vacuumed Ronny's footprints from the carpet.

When we came home there was nothing left of the Ronny we knew. I made such a mistake.

The Second Year

Experts on grief agree that a person is grieving "well" who eventually faces her grief in some way. Perhaps by talking. Crying. Writing. Releasing anger verbally, or through physical exercise. However grief is expressed, the loss should be faced by the second year. In other words, the period of shock should now be past, reality should be known, and improvements in daily functioning should be visible. The fleeting "good periods," where life is still experienced with some savor, should lengthen.

But there are tremendous fluctuations in the improvements of the second year. Some people make a considerable adjustment by then. They may plan to remarry, or be ready to give birth to (or adopt) another child. But that is not the norm for others.

For these others, even though daily functioning has improved (for example, returning to work, or caring with more enthusiasm for other children), the inner facing of the loss may only now be at its peak. The cushion of shock is gone, and only stark reality remains.

Many who grieve wake up one morning in the second year with the realization, "This is really my life. This is it. This *will be* it." Such inner truths cause the second year to be emotionally crushing. Pain is now being felt to its deepest extent.

This new, sharper pain is incredibly defeating. It's easy for the bereaved to conclude, "If after all this time now I'm doing worse, I'll *never* get better."

But the deeper pain and the stark reality actually herald progress. Pain must eventually be faced; healing demands it. So whenever pain is confronted, the healing process is gaining.

As a friend, don't withdraw your support after the first year. Even though the bereaved may have resumed her day-to-day functions, the inner awareness of loss may never be greater. Make allowance for this, and continue to create opportunities for her to talk. Also stretch your understanding, and allow for bleak moods and newly dampened spirits. She may need you in the second year as much as she did in the beginning stages of grief.

Don't Forget Your Friend

Too often a widow (or widower) finds herself "uninvited" to be with the same circle of couples she was a part of before the death of her spouse. Everyone surrounded her initially. But when others' lives returned to normal and social patterns resumed, the invitations gradually dwindled. This is less typical for senior citizens, but very typical when the widowed person is young. This sudden absence of invitations is hurtful—in strong terms it tells the widowed person that because she is all alone, she no longer fits in. Society prefers couples.

> *The greatest tragedy in life is what dies inside a man while he is still alive.*
>
> Albert Einstein

A widowed person can be successfully included at a gathering of couples if there is sensitivity and forethought. The most awkward moments usually surround issues like transportation and paying the bill in a restaurant. When I was asked and could state my preference honestly beforehand (e.g. "I'd like to ride with you so I won't have to drive alone," or "I'd like to pay you beforehand so you can handle my bill at the restaurant"), I was always more comfortable. I did *not* feel comfortable if I was treated like an invalid or always "treated" to the movie or meal. I felt enough like a fifth wheel in my widowhood without having my inclusion in a social evening cause more special treatment.

The sharpest hurt for widowed persons can be when friends surprise them with a date, the eligible man or woman who "just happens" to arrive as their dinner partner, or theater companion. Such surprises can be very demeaning, even if you, as a friend, had good intentions. It suggests that the companionship of a widowed person alone is not good enough. Your widowed friend might feel she must be part of a couple in order to be acceptable for a night out on the town. It may also backfire and suggest to the widow that you think her incapable of attracting a date on her own. The friend who arranges such a surprise never intends any of this, but it is a gesture which usually falls hard and flat.

You can help the most by being candid, simply asking what your friend prefers. Even if comfortable arrangements are not worked out, it matters significantly to your friend that you have asked. The invitation says clearly that she is not forgotten.

I was widowed for twelve years before remarrying, and I never felt completely comfortable joining couples for an evening when I was the only single person present. But it mattered a great deal to me to receive the invitations. It made me feel remembered, and helped to teach me that my social worth was not only as a duo. And sitting at home because I'd refused an invitation to join friends was a world apart from knowing that everyone was getting together and I hadn't been asked.

Creative Invitations

For me, the most helpful invitations were both candid and creative. They might have included a request that I'd join in with others as before; but if not, they offered other alternatives which might be more comfortable for me (perhaps seeing members of a couple separately, or meeting in a public place without the vivid reminders of anyone's home).

For parents who have lost their only child, there is also awkwardness in re-entering their old social world. They no longer relate as "family" in the same way, nor will they be participating anymore in the same activities. Two-parent families who have suddenly become one-parent families feel equally awkward. They wonder, "How will I fit in?"

You can help tremendously by issuing invitations and including these persons. Unpressured invitations, especially for the holidays, are lovely gifts. And if you do invite, it's an extra courtesy to tell your guest who will be there, and what the day is usually like. That always helped me to judge whether or not I'd be comfortable. When the invitation was also issued with the spoken understanding that I could accept or refuse until the last moment, I appreciated it doubly.

When I was living in Connecticut, the Robeys, the Bakers, the Gillespies, and the Judges invited my daughter Beth and me to join them and their families for different holidays over and over again. They told me who would be there and what their traditions and schedules were like. There was never any pressure on me to accept the invitation, and no sense of hurt if I refused. Often I already had plans, or sometimes I preferred to be alone. But I could say what I felt and know they would not stop inviting me. The times when Beth and I did join one of these families are rich memories. They probably will never know what their invitations meant. Even if I refused, staying at home when there had been other choices was totally different from staying at home because there was no place to go.

Friends Laura and Chuck further proved how creative and reaching love can be. When I was first widowed and left with an infant, they were newly married and had not yet begun their own family. Christmas morning was so stark for me, yet it was terribly important to me that Beth's Christmas mornings take place right in her own home. Laura and Chuck had no family nearby, so they offered to come to *me* on Christmas morning. For years I phoned them on that morning as soon as Beth was awake, at whatever hour, and they would arrive within minutes. Their presence helped me through the early Christmas hours in a way I could never repay. After a fancy breakfast they returned to their own home, and I could have the quiet I needed. The hardest hours were now behind me.

Had they invited me to be with them in *their* home I probably wouldn't have gone. I needed to be at my own house. So they—in loving, creative concern—came to me. What a gift that was! And still is—in my grateful memories.

Something to Think About . . .

As your friend works through her grief, especially in the first two years, in what creative ways can you be a support?

10
Other Poignant Losses

There are many types of grief and loss. But the one thing they all have in common is that the grieving ones desperately need the understanding and sensitivity of good friends. And this is especially true in the situations of miscarriage and suicide.

Miscarriage

Those who lose children through miscarriage, stillbirth, or new-born death often find that others do not recognize their loss to be as great as the loss of an older child, or even a real loss at all. In these circumstances in particular, the pain may be dismissed with the comment, "Don't worry, you'll have another child." The attitude of many seems to be, *Since the child wasn't known to you, how deep can the grief be?*

But the truth is that the child *is* well-known to the expectant parents who have anticipated the birth, and invested their hopes and love in the child's safe arrival. The loss is every bit as deep as other losses. In fact, the grief carries a particular poignancy because the parents have not only lost a child, but have lost that child without experiencing any fulfillment. Many never even held their baby, and will have no memories to comfort them. It is as if they have been robbed twice.

The mother especially is susceptible to the question, "What did I do wrong?" She is so tempted to consider herself unfit biologically, and to feel that she has failed.

A friend can help by understanding the depth of the loss. The couple *are* parents, and they *did* lose a child. They will, indeed, hurt. And although attention understandably flows primarily to the woman, who has physically borne the infant, the loss is different, but of no less significance, for the expectant father. Don't forget him—his dreams died, too.

Remember that these parents grieve in the same way that parents of an older child grieve. They will have the same helpless feelings, the same disappointment. In addition, when death results through miscarriage, they will remember throughout the months that follow at what stage they "would have been" in their pregnancy. When full-term birth would have occurred, it will be

And someday you'll learn . . . that the loss, the great emptiness of the cavern inside you, fills up with grief. It spills over so many times with tears. But if you cut the darkness loose every day, cut it loose, let it go with God, surrender it, and surrender even the surrender place, for one final time that happens over and over again, the darkness will spill out, and all that will be left will be the light.

Geoffrey Brown, "The Blessing Inside Sorrow"

a particularly difficult season. Reach out to them especially at this time.

Unmentionable Deaths

Survival of every loss is wounding. However, there is a special hurt known to those whose loved ones died by an act of suicide, or by any of the other so-called "unmentionable" deaths (e.g., drug-related, alcohol-related, AIDS, etc.). Survivors of these deaths may be heavily burdened by a sense of failure and responsibility, as well as a loss of self-esteem. Their hearts ache with the question, "What did I do wrong? How did I fail, that my loved one saw no hope?" Added to all the drama and grief is a deep sense of shame for the way death has occurred.

A friend can help by not pulling back. Don't be afraid to approach the bereaved, and be willing to listen if the shame can be voiced. For these survivors, death has dealt a double blow: the loss of the loved one, and the loss of their own self-confidence and respect. Those bereaved easily assume that others are judging them as parents or spouses, and that they fall short. So as a friend, affirm their gifts and their shining qualities. You will be a lifeline.

My friends Jim and Priscilla have survived their daughter Linda's suicide. They grieved as all parents grieve, and they felt that extra sense of shame and lowered confidence. Then, in conversation, the priest in their parish suggested that they would

---

Grief may be joy misunderstood.
Elizabeth Barrett Browning, "De Profundis"

---

be excellent candidates to be foster parents. Priscilla recalls that his affirmation was not only pleasing, but healing. It showed them that they still had value and worth as people and as parents. Their daughter's act did not devalue their gifts, nor their ability to love and nurture a child. One person's belief in them planted an important seed.

There are countless, similar creative ways for friends to affirm those who grieve over "unmentionable" deaths. Solicit their advice. Nominate them for positions of responsibility and trust. Ask them to teach or care for other youth. Even if your love does not seem to produce noticeable changes in the immediate future, persist. The healing power of love is greater than shame.

Grief Is Grief

Grief. Loss. There are so many variables that it is impossible to touch on them all. Life's losses aren't limited to the physical death of a spouse, child, or other family member. They can be loss of employment, death of a pet (which in many households is like a family member), infertility, divorce, or moving from a treasured house and place to unknown territory. And they include the losses caused by aging and disease—loss of bodily and mental control, physical signs of aging, etc. They can also be the traumatic death of dreams—a construction worker who works happily for ten years, falls and crushes his spine and remains, for the rest of his life, in a wheelchair.

Whatever life's losses are, large and small, they hit each one of us in an individual way. And we grieve. We mourn, and we go through many of the steps—anger, guilt, fear—on our road to healing and wholeness again.

Something to Think About . . .

Think of a friend who may be experiencing a less obvious loss than death, but a real loss, nonetheless. How can you help?

11
As Time
Goes On . . .

It's now been thirteen years since my loss, but one or two friends still drop me a note on the anniversary of my family's death. My mother also remembers to call. What rich gestures these are! They tell me that I do not remember alone and validate the importance of the people I lost.

Continue to Remember

The bereaved will always remember, even when her life has gone on very happily. The dates of the loss are indelible marks. When others remember too, the day is lightened.

As a friend (or as a church), consider keeping an informal calendar of the important dates surrounding someone's loss. Jot down the date and year of the death, also marking birthdays, anniversaries, and the period six months and one year following the loss. When the special days arrive, the calendar will remind you to pay a visit, write a card, call, send flowers, etc. Include days that the bereaved may tell you are especially difficult for her. Two or three words of remembrance have greater meaning than you will ever know.

Plant a Seed of Strength and Hope

About a year after my losses I had a brief meeting and conversation with Dr. Norman Vincent Peale, the beloved and internationally respected minister. I remember how fragile I felt as I walked into his office. The furniture seemed large and consuming, and Dr. Peale's own presence felt imposing. I know today that his office furniture is no different in size than the sofa in my living room. Nor is Dr. Peale anyone to regard with fright. But my perceptions on that first visit were colored by the terror within me. Grief distorts the way a bereaved person views her environment, and few places seem safe.

Dr. Peale talked with me kindly and prayed. I was broken and deeply wounded, still reeling with my pain. But one line from our conversation kept echoing in my heart. Dr. Peale had said to me, "Paula, I believe you will overcome this."

Six words. *I believe you will overcome this.* I hardly believed the words at that moment, but I wished them to be true. With all my heart, I wished them to be true. And their powerful effect was to plant a seed of hope and belief within me.

In succeeding years I have sat with hundreds of other grieving parents or widows who, like me, thought they would never recover from the blow of death. I've looked into many defeated eyes. And in my own way I've tried to pass on the great gift Dr. Peale gave to me. I've told these survivors that pain is not the final say. If they choose to do so, they *can* heal.

As a friend to one who grieves, you cannot choose for her. But you can plant seeds with your words that will give the bereaved every advantage. You can remind her of her strength, and of the power of God which is within her. You can remind her that there is healing equal to her pain. You can speak words which summon the best in all of us:

> I believe in you.
> God will give you the strength that it takes.
> I believe you will overcome this.

When an image of someone's best self is lovingly presented to her through the eyes of another, from deep within she may be stirred to become that self.

Remind Her That She Has Choices

Death can change dreams. It may thwart plans and rob its survivors of their innocence. And whether it is accepted graciously, or by kicking and screaming all the rest of life, when someone has grieved, she is changed—forever.

Many who grieve say, "I will never get over this." But that is not true. Going on is a choice. The circumstances which brought about the grief can never be altered. But what she does next—how she decides to live the rest of her life—is up to her. Healing is ultimately not a divine act alone, nor a chance of fate. Healing

---

Finally, a remarkable thing begins to happen. You notice that for short periods the hurt is not so great. This is the beginning of your healing.

Sharan Morris, in Haddon W. Robinson's *Grief*

---

is a choice of the will. And sometimes it takes a courageous friend to help the bereaved face that truth.

This is part of a letter which Allan and Lois, as grieving parents, received from their close friend, Cubby.

> You have been in my thoughts constantly. There are so many things in my life which I have been able to square away neatly—complete with how and why—but Emily's death is not one of them . . .
>
> I don't think your pain is being caused by the thought that Emily has been erased—am I right? You and I know for a fact that Emily still exists—in another room in God's great house. What I would guess is that your pain comes from being suddenly left with an overwhelming volume of love—and no one to give it to. Sort of like those full breasts of yours, Lois, and all that milk.
>
> The milk will go to waste. The love will not . . . I would guess that the best way to dissipate the love would be to break it up into small pieces and give it away. Knowing you two, that will not be difficult. You will give it away piece by piece, and every time you do you will say quietly, "Here. This is from Emily and me."

It's never that someone who grieves can't love again, or be happy again. It's that they either will, or they won't.

Nearly three years after my losses, I was still living in my past, handcuffed to my memories. I'd made sizable outer adjustments, but in my heart I was still tied to yesterday. And then my friend Paul confronted me with just that truth. "You see yourself as a grieving widow and mother," he said, "and nothing more. You're not choosing to live your life today. You've given up on the person you were meant to be."

His words wounded me and angered me. How dare he? How dare he criticize me at all when life had dealt me such blows? I didn't want to be challenged; I wanted to be comforted. I thought I deserved to be comforted. It took me a long while before I understood that his words were not filled with judgment, but love.

As a friend, you may have to voice a loving challenge, like Paul's to me. If your words are motivated by love, the hearer will know (even if, initially, she reacts in anger). But understand that you can only speak the challenge. At best you can be the facilitator for your friend's choices, but you will not be able to make the choices *for* her. You cannot give life to another person. Each journeyer can only give life to herself.

Madeleine L'Engle taught me that "grief doesn't leave you. You leave grief." And when I heard Paul's challenge to leave my grief and live as if I were alive in the present day, I set in motion the final stages of healing.

And that may be the greatest miracle about us: We are capable of finding new keys to living in the present. *Always.* We can dream many dreams.

How can you help a friend who is grieving? Love her as she grieves—listen to her—be patient—accept her as she is—and

> ... *death is but one aspect of experience, a phase of life in transition . . . It is small wonder that spring and Easter merge into a glorious expression of the aliveness of life.*
>
> Howard Thurman, *Deep Is the Hunger*

believe that pain, in spite of its sting, can be a great teacher. Grief can be transformative for those with open hearts, for when you are cut open by grief, God can enter. Friends who build a bridge of love to one who is grieving become the bearers of God. The arms, hands, and listening hearts of friends have the power to carry the hope of purpose beyond pain—purpose which no loss can destroy. And the love and acceptance of friends create the most favorable environment in which one who grieves may look within and find for herself that if you know God, nothing has the power to defeat you.

Something to Think About . . .

Today is the day to plant a seed of strength and hope for your friend.

Epilogue

Grief has been my great teacher. Its primary gifts to me have been a deep and abiding faith in God, an awareness that the present moments of life matter deeply, and a knowing that my everyday choices are powerful. Through them I either affirm life, or I do not.

Grief has taught me to cling to nothing—except my hope in God. To reject nothing, but to learn from everything. These lessons are continuous echoes on my journey.

Through death we all will eventually lose the presence of those whom we love. We will lose the expression of that love in tangible form. But we won't lose love.

The very grief that wounded me has made me rich. And if you have loved someone through the grieving process, the deep lessons of grief are also yours.

Resources

Support Groups

Communities around the world offer support groups for the bereaved. Such groups are based on the principle that no one understands like someone who has been there. They offer the bereaved an opportunity to share freely with others in similar circumstances, and the help provided by such groups can be invaluable.

For parents who have lost children:

The Compassionate Friends, Inc.
National Headquarters
P.O. Box 3696
Oak Park, IL 60522
630/990-0010
Sponsors local chapters for parents who have lost children, surviving siblings, survivors of infant death and miscarriage.

For young widows and widowers:

THEOS (They Help Each Other Spiritually)
Theos International Foundation, Inc.

Suite 105
322 Blvd. of the Allies
Pittsburgh, PA 15222-1919
Local chapters in many states.

Community support groups for the bereaved are also sponsored by local clinics, hospitals, social service organizations, and churches.

Counseling

Counseling services are widely available for those who grieve. This can be a crucial step for many to take as they struggle with grief's phases. Even for those who are facing their grief successfully, it is a great benefit to seek a counselor's support. Far from being a sign of weakness, the step to seek counseling during the grief process is a wise sign of strength. Those who are helped through grief's difficult terrain increase their likelihood of emerging from the grief experience with greater strength and understanding, and a deeper healing. Look in your yellow pages under Counseling Services, or contact your local church for references. Many pastors are also good one-on-one counselors.

Reading List

Bayly, Joe, *The Last Thing We Talk About* (David C. Cook, 1969).

Brooks, Anne M., *The Grieving Time* (Harmony Books, 1985). An honest, once-a-month journal written by a middle-aged widow. Her entries are brief and piercingly real.

Hsu, Dorothy, *Mending* (Christian Literature Crusade, 1982). A widow's diary of her first year alone. Her thoughts and emotions are candid, and her calling out to God is unquestionably sincere.

LeShan, Eda, *Learning to Say Good-by: When a Parent Dies* (Avon, 1976). A simple direct look at the fears and feelings which children experience when a parent dies. Written for the whole family.

Mellonie, Bryan, and Robert Ingpen, *Lifetimes: The Beautiful Way to Explain Death to Children* (Bantam, 1983). Beautifully illustrated, clear, and simple enough for children of all ages and parents, too.

Robinson, Haddon W., *Grief* (Zondervan, 1976).

Shaw, Luci, *God in the Dark* (Zondervan, 1989).

Worden, Mary Jane, *Early Widow: A Journal of the First Year* (Inter-Varsity Press, 1989). A young widow's journal which addresses honestly the shock of grief and the struggle to cope with three children's grief as well as her own. Her story is beautifully told and filled with rich insights and suggestions.

Bibliography

Bayly, Joe, *The Last Thing We Talk About* (David C. Cook, 1969).

Brown, Geoffrey, "The Blessing Inside Sorrow, " n.p.

Cleland, Max, *Strong at the Broken Places* (Berkley Books, 1982).

Dickinson, Emily, *The Complete Poems of Emily Dickinson* (Little, Brown, & Co., 1980).

Gibran, Kahil, *The Prophet* (Alfred A. Knopf, 1965).

Graham, Billy, *Facing Death* (Grason, 1987).

Hansel, Tim, *You Gotta Keep Dancin'* (David C. Cook, 1985).

Helson, Judy, The Compassionate Friends, Inc., *The Providence, Rhode Island chapter newsletter.*

Keller, Helen, *The Story of My Life* (New American Library, 1988).

Lapierre, Dominique, *The City of Joy* (Warner Books, 1985).

Robinson, Haddon W., *Grief* (Zondervan, 1976).

Thurman, Howard, *Deep Is the Hunger* (Friends United Press, 1951).

Watson, David, *Fear No Evil* (Shaw Publishers, 1985).

Williams, Margery, *The Velveteen Rabbit* (Doubleday, 1922).